G000088483

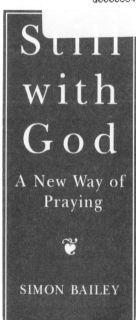

Still
with
God

A New Way of
Praying

SIMON BAILEY

National Society/Church House Publishing
Church House, Great Smith Street, London SW1P 3NZ

For Caroline, Jason, Steven, Christopher and Mervyn

This book would not have been possible without the Revd John Hudson, the Revd Molly Kenyon - and most of all Brother Kenneth CGA

ISBN 0 7151 4828 1

First published in 1986 for the General Synod Board of Education. Second revised edition first published in 1993 by The National Society and Church House Publishing

Reprinted 1996

The National Society (Church of England) for Promoting Religious Education is a charity which supports everyone involved in Christian education. It publishes a wide range of books and booklets, and two magazines *Crosscurrent* and *Together with Children.*

For further details please contact the Promotions Secretary, The National Society, Church House, Great Smith Street, London SW1P 3NZ.

Cover design by Julian Smith
Printed in England by Orphans Press

CONTENTS

THINGS TO REMEMBER
ABOUT PRAYING

(You'll only need to read this once . . .)

Sometimes praying is wonderful –
enjoy it when it is.

Most of the time it's hard work,
never let anyone tell you that it isn't.
There will be times when praying seems impossible
– keep at it if you can.
Try to pray at least for a few moments every day,
or if that's too hard, at least every week.

Sometimes of course it will be wonderful.

Remember

– You never pray on your own:
  someone somewhere will be praying with you –
  if not on earth then in heaven.
  (Just think of all those saints . . .)

– Praying isn't words.
  Praying is discovering the presence of God –
  finding that he's there waiting for you anyway.

– Relax. Be still.
  Wait for him as often as you can.
  Don't worry how others pray –
  you only need the things that work for you.
  When it's time to move on to
  a new way of praying, you'll know –
  and God will be waiting for you there.

Matthew tells us that
Jesus said: 'Pray in secret,'
on your own and out of sight.
He also said: 'Don't babble on' –
a very few words will do;
and then he gave his friends
his own prayer – 'Our Father . . .'
You can't do better than that.
Use that prayer every day –
sometimes, if you do it slowly,
you'll need nothing else.

(See Matthew 6.7)

Our Father in heaven,
hallowed be your name,
your kingdom come,
your will be done,
on earth as in heaven.

Give us today our daily bread.

Forgive us our sins
as we forgive those who sin against us.
Lead us not into temptation
but deliver us from evil.

For the kingdom, the power, and the glory
are yours
now and for ever.
Amen.

Somebody said there are only two
other Christian prayers – both very small,
both used by millions through the ages.
They're a good place to start.

ALLELUIA

LORD HAVE MERCY

PRAYERS WHEN EVERYTHING IS ALL RIGHT

Alleluia

Alleluia is the song-prayer of Easter:
the Church's shout of joy for the risen Jesus.
It comes from a Jewish cry of praise
long before the time of Jesus – 'Hallelujah'.
It means 'Praise the Lord'.
We use it as the special song of joy,
during the fifty days from Easter to
   Whitsun especially –
it sums up in one word
our delight that Jesus is alive
our joy in living
all the excitement of new life
which faith gives us.
Alleluia!
Go on – say it – alleluia!
Over and over again –
Alleluia! Alleluia! Alleluia! . . .

Today, God, I can't stop laughing.
It's not that everything is funny
just that everything feels happy.
I keep smiling at people –
and it makes them laugh as well
(though some of them give me
very funny looks . . .)

Yesterday at the dentist
I didn't feel like laughing –
I know I can't always be happy
but today I am happy and laughing
so I'll keep on smiling.

I keep bubbling over – it's your doing:
you are making me happy, God –
you are the gladness,
you're the one who keeps making me laugh,
and somehow when I laugh
I think I can hear you laughing as well.
It's lovely.

Everything hinges on Easter:
it's the absolute centre of everything.
An early Christian writer said:
'If Christ was not raised,
then our good news is empty and so is
your faith – we turn out to be
lying witnesses for God.'

Easter means that death is not the end –
it was not the end for Jesus.
It can never be the end for anyone
ever again!
There is something more than death,
something deeper, something bigger –
Jesus has been there.

It's so new, so different, so full of life
it's hard to grasp.
All we can do is shout Alleluia!
That way we challenge death
every day of our lives.

(See 1 Corinthians 15. 14)

Little Easters

I'm singing Alleluia so loudly inside of me!
It's Sunday again, God, and I can feel
all the life of Easter springing up!

Every Sunday is a little Easter.
There are friends to meet, songs to sing,
new life in the bread and wine,
a new day, a new week, nothing spoilt yet!

I'm glad, God, to be one of your people –
we're spread out all over the world –
and in the next one too –
filled with Christ's new life.
Father, our Father,
I can almost feel them around me:
together, all of us, we are your Easter people.

And here in church we'll hear again
the words that make us 'Easter people' –
words of Jesus,
words vibrating with such joy
– everything would be so empty without Easter.
Alleluia!

By baptism we become part of Easter –
joined to Christ in his dying and rising:
no longer on our own,
all of us part of him,
for ever.
It's a kind of drowning to make us alive.

All baptisms used to take place at Easter –
people would go to a river before dawn on
Easter day dressed in their old clothes.
They would wait in the Great Vigil on
that 'night of nights' while the church told
the whole story of Christ dying and rising,
and then they would be baptised, plunged
in the water, coming out to be robed in Easter
white and to make their first Communion,
as the sun rose.

Easter belongs to every Christian –
in this great celebration
we remember our baptism and
the day we put on Christ.

Taking the Plunge

Now that I can swim, God,
I like the deep end best.
I like to hold my nose
and try to touch the bottom –
but I keep my eyes open
so I can see all that water.

I think you are something like a swimming pool.
When I hear bits of Paul's letters
he keeps talking about being 'in Christ'
and I think he means something like that.

You're a pool that we dive into by baptism
and we're all joined together –
joined to him – by the water.
It's such great water – better than the baths –
so warm, so clear, so deep.

(See Philippians 2.1, Romans 6.3)

With your People

I'm glad about my church.
Sometimes it seems stuffy –
but I know I need other people.
We need to be together,
knock each other's corners off,
even try to love each other.
Jesus said that.
'Love each other.'
It's hard work but I know it's right.

So –
I'll start right here, while I'm praying –
although I can't love everyone around just yet,
praying for people is one way to start loving them.

Thank you for all of them: one day,
if we work at it, and with your help,
we really shall be one people –
just what you want us to be.

(See John 13. 34)

With your Universe

Everything is so beautiful:
absolutely everything seems to be singing and glad.
It's all shouting 'Yes!', Father, to you –
'You've got it right! It's okay!'

Jesus shouted Yes to you
– or, putting it the other way round
like Paul does,
Jesus is *your* Yes to us –
You accept us, agree with us,
you are on our side.

I want to join the universe
in saying Yes to you as well.
The singer of the psalms
was always saying Yes to you,
Mary said Yes when the angel came to her,
Jesus said his Yes the hard way,
on the cross,
and now I want to say my Yes as well;
I want to join in *their* great affirmation,
we can say it together:
'Yes, we're on the same side!'
AMEN!

('Amen' *means* 'let it be so. Yes!')
(See II Corinthians 1. 19,20)

There are so many things to be glad about,
that deserve an alleluia all of their own,
you must have plenty of them . . .

Here are two blank pages for your own prayers.

(If you write them in pencil you can always rub them
out when you change your mind . . .)

Hoping

Jesus, were you wasting your time
talking with such excitement
about the 'kingdom of God',
about a new kind of government,
a beautiful society?
You must have believed it could happen.
You force us to hope that one day
it will come – free, open, full of love:
help us to work hard for it with you.
Then one day . . . one day
our Father's kingdom *will* come
on earth as in heaven.

In *your* imagination, Jesus,
what was 'the kingdom' like?
Like a tree in spring grown from a tiny seed,
like long lost children with their fathers,
like a wonderful, long and happy party . . .
But I think it will be like
one of those spectacular TV shows
where absolutely everyone
is instantly given their heart's desire
absolutely free –
It'll take our breath away.
I'm looking forward to that . . .

PRAYERS WHEN THINGS ARE NOT SO GOOD

Lord Have Mercy

'Lord have mercy' was the other prayer
we started with, as old and as well-used
as Alleluia
It began in the Greek language as
'kyrie eleison' and sometimes that is still said
at the beginning of Holy Communion.

Alleluia is all very well
but we simply aren't glad all the time –
there are lots of things that make us miserable,
in ourselves
and in the world around us:
all of them push us back onto God for help.

If Alleluia is the song on one side of Easter,
Lord have mercy is on the other . . .

Good Friday

I've got this cross on a chain, Jesus,
to hang round my neck – you're on it –
nailed there.
It's disgusting –
a human being fixed on a cross.
What was it all for?
Why do we remember something so horrible?
And we don't just remember it,
we call it the most important thing of all:
we put it up everywhere.

Is the cross so important because this way
you can take hold of us right at the very worst
of the mess we get ourselves into
and lift us out?
You can only do it by getting in here with us.

You love us that much?

Is it something to do with your wanting
to share everything that we go through,
no matter how sad or painful or ugly?

Something like that anyway.

You *know* what it's like –
friends all gone, unbearable pain,
failure and defeat – you've been there.
You *know* what crying out 'Lord have mercy'
really means.
You – of all people – thought
that God had deserted you
completely.

Perhaps I take my little cross
too much for granted –
but at least it makes me think about you
some of the time.

When we cry out 'have mercy'
we know straight away,
because of Good Friday,
that God listens and understands:
that's why we call it *Good* Friday.

Unlike the stories of Easter,
the story of the last days of Jesus
is much the same in all the gospels –
especially in Matthew, Mark and Luke –
check it for yourself.

It's a solemn, haunting story
that slowly spirals down to its end
on the cross.
We can feel Jesus gradually
taking all our miseries,
all the things that hurt,
on with him to the cross
where for ever he cries out, for us –
'Lord have mercy!'

(See Matthew 26. 27, Mark 14. 15, Luke 22. 23, John 18. 19)

Our story

The film was fun tonight, God.
We seem to need lots of stories,
we're always telling them, reading them,
and watching them on TV,
keeping up with them in magazines and comics.
Everybody seems to need stories.

You give us a story too – a true one –
a story that draws everything together
like a lens pulling everything into focus.
That last week of his life –
step by step to crucifixion –
is riveting.
Step by step I feel
nearer to him,
feel him watching *me*
when he turns to look at Peter,
comforting *me*
when he meets the weeping people of Jerusalem,
including *me*
when he speaks from his pain on the cross.

This story is big enough to hold me too
– and not just sad after all –
there's something else as well,
on the other side.

'Lord have mercy' sums up
all our prayers of sadness.
Prayers out of pain,
prayers when we've hurt other people,
prayers when the world seems
so ugly and mean and out of control,
prayers when we or anything else fall short
of being 'good', of being a glad 'yes!'

Remember again:
Good Friday means we can know that
God hears us straight away.
We pray *through* the Christ of Good Friday
(we are 'in him', remember)
that's why *all* our prayers end like that:
'Through Jesus Christ, our Lord. Amen.'
(Add it yourself to the prayers of this book.)

Here are some prayers
to channel through Christ to God:

I'm miserable . . .

It's not that it's all going wrong, Father,
though some things could be better;
and I *know* there are lots of people
worse off than me
(they keep telling me that)
but I'm just miserable.

For no real reason I'm fed up
with everything and everybody –
I feel as if I'm down at the bottom of a pit,
sunk in the mud and,
like a bad dream,
I can't lift myself out.
But *you* can.

The singer of the psalms was fed up,
he asked you to lift him up –
will you lift me up too?
(I know you can.)

(See Psalms 88 and 40)

I'm sorry . . .

God, I've been so mean.
I felt as if I couldn't help it
(but maybe I could have).
All day I've been
cruel and spiteful and nasty and mean
(and lonely).
Now I'm sorry.

I'm horrible sometimes:
I don't like myself very much –
but I know I don't have to behave this way.
When I get round to being *really* sorry
it all feels different:
I want to be with people, to make friends
and help them. I feel then as if I'm living again.

So I *am* sorry – saying sorry to you
helps me to feel sorry to *everyone*
(but I'll try to say it to them too).
Somehow I can give you all the hurt
I've spread around, and you take it away.
(But even then there are some things
I've spoilt for good – forgive me for them.)

I'll go wrong again, I know I will,
but now I am truly sorry.

I'm puzzled

So many of my friends say they don't
believe in you, Lord, it puzzles me.
How do I know it's all true?
Isn't it all a bit much?
You can feel a long way off –
so far off I think you may not be there at all.

It gets very hard.
(They laugh at me sometimes.)
Some of your first followers found it hard too:
so hard they went away –
you asked your closest friends if
they were going too:
Peter said: 'Where else can we go?
You have the words of eternal life'.

I like that – I like Peter for that:
there *isn't* anywhere else to go –
even when, after all, Peter denied you in the end
he still came back to you
(and you helped him say he loved you).

However hard it is, however puzzled I get,
I still stay here with you –
clinging on by my fingernails sometimes –
because there isn't anywhere else to go:
you give us life.

(See John 6.68)

I'm frightened . . .

There were wars and riots on the news tonight,
Father, and now I'm very frightened –
bombs and killings and rows don't seem *too* bad
in the daylight, but it's dark now . . .
I don't let other people know I'm frightened
of the dark but I am.
I'm scared of lots of things –
evil spirits and heights, being beaten up,
pain and dying,
and even just looking silly in front of my friends.
Now I'm scared of going to sleep in case I dream.

Be near me,
be a warm presence round me
and a light inside me.
You know what it's like to be very scared,
so you can help me now.
I'm nearly shivering with fright,
so help me to know you are in charge,
you know what darkness is,
you are brighter than the darkness
and warm enough to take all my shivers away.

I'm tired . . .

I saw a tramp leaning on the bus stop, Jesus,
and he looked tired out –
so many people are tired,
even I feel tired sometimes.

You could be exhausted too, but you
went away to rest
on your own –
not talking, not working, not even thinking –
just resting.
And then you said:
'Come to me, if you're tired, and rest.'
We're all so tired –
the rest of the world as much as I am.
So – even if we can't get away as you did –
we'll just have to take up your invitation,
come to you,
and rest.

(See Matthew 11. 28-30)

PRAYERS EXPLORING WHO I AM, WHAT I WANT, WHERE I'M GOING

Growing Prayers

Not all our prayers are clear-cut –
'Alleluia' or 'Lord have mercy'.
We find ourselves praying about
who we are and how we feel,
neither altogether glad nor altogether sad,
but reaching out in between –
wondering, hoping and longing,
asking and exploring –
reaching for God.

(You'll notice, perhaps,
that the Holy Spirit comes in here
sometimes in a special way –
He is the Spirit of growing,
our encourager and our supporter.)

Me

Father,
it's strange to know
that I'm growing and changing all the time.
All my friends are changing too,
not just their clothes but their shape,
their voices.
The way we think,
the things we think about.

When it feels strange and different,
remind me then that
you are growing with me –
your Spirit is closer to me
than my own body,
nearer to me than my own heart-beat:
all the strangeness and the fear
and the wonder is yours.
To be growing and alive is to be like you,
to be part of you.

God's Family

You're a sort of family, God,
(but a better one than all of ours)
you're *so* close that you're all one,
Father, Son and Holy Spirit –
but within that closeness
you make each other totally free as well.
'Holy Trinity' is a picture of freedom –
total trust and single-minded love.

Something like that, anyway.

Help me to see why I need my family,
help us to be more like you,
help us to make each other free.

God, my Mother

Our Mother;
can I call you that?
Sometimes, God, you feel just like my mother –
only more so.
I can trust you,
take you for granted,
depend on you – and you're there.
Just like waking from a nightmare,
crying out and she's there to hold me,
saying: 'Everything's going to be all right'.

Jesus said you, God, are like a mother hen,
gathering her chicks to brood over them,
protecting them,
to make them warm,
to make them live:
sometimes it feels just like that.

Thank you, my Mother.

(See Luke 13. 34)

Part of the crowd

I don't want to be different, God,
I want to be part of the crowd –
accepted, liked, one of them.
But there are some things I *don't* want to do.
I have to be different and go off on my own.
Help me to know when it's right
to stand apart from the crowd;
it's no use being different
just to gain attention.
Help me to know myself a bit better
when I have to make decisions.

Thank you for my special friends

especially ....
for the interests and jokes we share.
Jesus knew how important friends were,
he talked things through with his friends
and cared for them so deeply –
help me to be like them,
and maybe, God,
I can call *you* 'Friend' as well.

Sex

What do you think about page three, God?
You made her after all –
and you made sex.
But I don't think you made it dirty and cheap
and that's what we often turn it into.

I don't really know
what to do with sex, God.
I know it's strong and powerful.
I know it's part of love.
I think it can be beautiful.
Help me to get past
all the dirt that's put in the way
and help me
to find you here as well.

One World

Butterflies and mountains, cities and seas,
people – trees – animals – machines –
they *all* come out of you in the end.
Maker, my Maker, you shaped it all –
including me –
to be one vast and delicate whole,
everything linked to everything else,
enjoying everything else.

And there you are, hiding in it all,
waiting and hoping to be found,
like a game of hide and seek –
you are secretly waiting,
overflowing wherever things live and grow.

Have mercy when we spoil the world,
when we wear it out, damage it, use it wrongly;
help us, like you, to cherish the world,
to discover you
in all the thousand places where you hide.

Change the World

We make such a mess of the world –
God, I want to do something!
Quarrelling, spoiling things, hurting each other –
I want to shake the world,
tell it not to be so stupid!
So many people are poor and hungry,
dying because they need food and water,
dying because they've lost all hope,
while the rest of us are so comfortable.
I want to *do* something.

Jesus said we can meet him
in every other person –
I want to live in a world
that treats *everyone* as if they were Jesus.
So help me to change the world:
I'll start now – with myself.
Fill me up with your Holy Spirit
and we'll start changing me –
I'll begin to treat everyone as if they were Jesus.

(See Matthew 25. 40)

Peace

They say we can destroy the world
twenty times over with nuclear bombs
it's probably more by now.
I see those pictures of the mushroom cloud
and I shiver –
the world is too beautiful for that,
people are too beautiful.
Father, it's so wrong – and so frightening.

Jesus told us to love our enemies –
I don't think you can love your enemies
with a bomb.
It's such a mess but somehow, somewhere
we have to turn round and *really* say:
'We want to live in peace together'.

So send your Spirit to remind our leaders
how beautiful things are,
how beautiful their 'enemies' are,
to remind them to keep telling themselves:
'We want to live in peace together'.

(See Matthew 5. 44)

Looking for mystery

Dracula and werewolves were on TV tonight.
I know they're not real, but I like
the strangeness and the mystery
they hint at.

In other places and at other times
I seem to feel a much deeper mystery:
sometimes in holy places,
sometimes reading about holy people –
or meeting them –
but sometimes it could be anywhere:
a feeling of awe and wonder comes over me,
like a huge dark tunnel opening up –
maybe you are the bright point of light
at the other end.
We so often fumble through our prayers
to find you,
it's good sometimes
to meet you like this.

For Holy Communion

Lord have mercy.

I know I'm going to meet you here
in the words I hear,
in the people I join with,
in the bread and wine.
I can feel your brightness
beginning to shine already –
it's showing up the shadows all over me:
have mercy because I've hurt people,
have mercy because I've hurt you,
come and scatter the shadows.

Lift up my head
so I can stand with your people
and meet you,
to receive you and feed on you.
Then we'll all be filled
with the warm brightness of your Holy Spirit,
(down inside like the wine)
able to sing out, at the tops of our voices,
Alleluia! Alleluia!

Jobs and no jobs

Perhaps I could have a sports car
one day, God;
something really fast and exciting.
For that I suppose I'll need a job
with lots of money,
and sometimes it doesn't look as though
I'll get a job at all.
Somehow we should be able to share
things out a bit more equally.
We need your Spirit to guide our thinking.

Some people work too hard,
they never have any fun,
while so many are depressed
because they can't work at all.
We ought to be able to do both –
work *and* have fun
(maybe work itself could even be fun . . .?)
It's very difficult – guide us, Spirit,
lead us towards a happier, freer, fairer world –
teach us to enjoy work, teach us how to share.

I'm prepared to do without my sports car
if it means more people can be happier and free.

Choices

I have to make so many choices
it's worse than a supermarket.
The older I get, Jesus, the more I'm on my own,
the more decisions I seem to have to make.
What to buy,
what clothes to wear today,
what to spend my money on . . .
And worse –
I have to choose what to think,
who to believe,
who to disagree with – and how;
choosing how to treat people,
when to agree with my friends,
when to be different –
decisions, decisions, decisions . . .

You made choices too.
Send your Spirit of right choices
to be *my* spirit,
and together we'll go on sorting out
the best way for me to go.

Death

People go all quiet and peculiar
when somebody dies:
I know why –
just thinking about it makes me feel strange:
once they were moving,
laughing, talking, alive –
now there's nothing there, all gone.

We all die – even me, though I feel so alive.
We're all afraid of dying –
that's part of the strangeness.

I can't imagine what happens 'after' death –
but somehow I feel life and love can be
stronger even than death, bigger and more real:
life and loving can swallow death.

That's what Jesus did –
ate up death with his love –
his new life swallowed death whole
and that's what *we're* all about too.
Death doesn't go away,
but you've taken out its poison –
life *is* stronger.

(See I Corinthians, 15. 54, II Corinthians 5. 4)

PRAYING FOR OTHERS

Praying also means holding up to God
people in need – family, friends, the sick, the poor.
We want to name them, remember them,
ask things for them – all of them.

There may be many people you want to pray for
and you won't be able to remember them all
every day.
You can try to pray for a different one –
or two – each day of the week,
or even spread over a month.

Try to think about them during the day too
rather than just ticking them off
on a list.
Think about them especially
if you're going to Holy Communion.

Today	I pray for:	
Sunday		
Monday		
Tuesday		
Wednesday		
Thursday		
Friday		
Saturday		

But don't worry too much if you forget them –
God doesn't forget.

OTHER THINGS ABOUT PRAYING

Praying isn't words, remember.
All sorts of other things are ways of praying too.
Here are some you can try:

Light a candle, let the flame –
alive and warm – become your prayer.

Use a picture or cross to help you 'focus':
something to look at –
a way of praying with your eyes.

Use your body as you pray.
Kneel; spread out your hands;
lie prostrate; maybe even dance
(King David did . . .)
Our bodies are praying as well as our minds.

One special movement your body can use is the sign
of the cross – you use your hand to cover yourself
with the cross-shape, a reminder that you belong 'in
Christ'. Or you can spread out your arms in the shape
of crucifixion.

(See II Samuel 6. 14)

You can use a piece of string
to help you to pray . . .
if you tie knots spaced along the string,
you say a short prayer
when you reach a knot,
as you pull the string
through your fingers:
it helps you to concentrate.
Many people all over the world
pray in this way.

Here are some short prayers to say with your string:

Lord have mercy.

Jesus is Lord.

Lord, you know that I love you.

You can make your own short prayers,
use single words (like the name of 'Jesus')
or use the ancient prayer:

Jesus, son of God, have mercy on me.

Don't be afraid of repetition – it helps.
And don't be afraid of saying your prayers
aloud when you can.

Many people like to go to special places
to pray – to holy places, shrines, where they feel
the love and the mystery of God.
Find a holy place near you
and go on a pilgrimage with your friends –
find your *own* holy place,
which might not be a church at all
but just a spot special to you.

There are probably certain men and women
you admire very much – saints of the Church,
whether they're called 'saint' or not:
thinking about them,
trying to follow them,
can also help you to pray.

The best thing of all to help our prayers
is Holy Communion.

Music can be praying too –
here we leave words behind altogether
and our hopes and fears
and our loves are shown,
without them,
in the music that moves us.

And at the end we come to silence –
praying isn't words
sometimes it needs to be total silence,
emptying ourselves,
saying nothing.

SILENCE

I know these are words I'm using
but really I'm trying to get away from them,
to go beyond all words and find you
in silence.
This book is full of words
but now I'm climbing above them.

There *are* some moments that are so quiet
that they fill up completely with you –
you alone.
I'm trying to reach
for one of those places now –
take away all the words,
take away every noise,
take away if you can
(yes, you can)
every thought as well.

It's strange
but I feel as if
I can stop talking *to* you
and simply be *with* you.

I want to be quite empty,
quite still,
and then you can come
slowly, gently,
filling me with yourself.

Come then, now –
the words end here.

AND AFTER ALL THAT . . .

Never forget that it's not those
who mouth words at God
who are the real followers of Jesus.
It's those who *love* like he did.

(See Matthew 7. 21)